WILD WORK

WHO SWINGS THE WRECKING BALL?

WORKING ON A BUILDING SITE

Mary Meinking

www.raintreepublishers.co.uk
Visit our website to find out more information about Raintree books.

To order:
☎ Phone 0845 6044371
🖹 Fax +44 (0) 1865 312263
🖳 Email myorders@raintreepublishers.co.uk

Customers from outside the UK please telephone +44 1865 312262

Raintree is an imprint of Capstone Global Library Limited, a company incorporated in England and Wales having its registered office at 7 Pilgrim Street, London, EC4V 6LB – Registered company number: 6695582

Edited by David Andrews, Nancy Dickmann, and Rebecca Rissman
Designed by Victoria Allen
Picture research by Liz Alexander
Leveled by Marla Conn, with Read-Ability.
Originated by Dot Gradations Ltd
Printed and bound in China by Leo Paper Products

ISBN 978 1 4062 1682 0 (hardback)
14 13 12 11 10
10 9 8 7 6 5 4 3 2 1

British Library Cataloguing in Publication Data
Meinking, Mary.
  Who swings the wrecking ball? : working on a building site.
  -- (Wild work)
  1. Construction workers--Juvenile literature.
  I. Title II. Series
  690'.023-dc22

Acknowledgements
The author and publisher are grateful to the following for permission to reproduce copyright material: Alamy pp. 15 (© Dan Leeth), 17 (© [apply pictures]), 21 (© Ken Welsh); Corbis pp. 4 (© Michael Reynolds/epa), 7 (© Andy Kingsbury), 24 (© Lance Nelson/Stock Photos), 25 (© Jack Hollingsworth), 27 (© Don Mason); Getty Images pp. 20 (Joel Rogers/Stone), 22 (Lester Lefkowitz/Stone); Masterfile Corporation p. 9 (Boden/Ledingham); Photolibrary pp. 12 (White), 13 (John Lund/Drew Kelly/Blend Images), 14 (Ralph Kerpa/imagebroker.net), 16 (Gary Moon/age footstock), 23 (Steve Dunwell/Index Stock Imagery), 26 (Chris Windsor/White), 28 (Granger Wootz/Blend Images); Shutterstock pp. 5 (© Anton Gvozdikov), 6 (© djgis), 8 (© 4634093993), 10 (© Doug Stevens), 11 (© Doug Stevens), 18 (© Faraways), 19 (© Khafizov Ivan Harisovich), 29 (© Feraru Nicolae).

Background design features reproduced with permission of Shutterstock (©Xtremer).

Cover photograph reproduced with permission of Corbis (©Construction Photography).

Every effort has been made to contact copyright holders of material reproduced in this book. Any omissions will be rectified in subsequent printings if notice is given to the publisher.

All the Internet addresses (URLs) given in this book were valid at the time of going to press. However, due to the dynamic nature of the Internet, some addresses may have changed, or sites may have changed or ceased to exist since publication. While the author and publisher regret any inconvenience this may cause readers, no responsibility for any such changes can be accepted by either the author or the publisher.

Some words are shown in bold, **like this**. You can find out what they mean by looking in the glossary.

Contents

From the ground up

Grab your hardhat for a look at building sites. Building is dangerous work. Sparks fly, wheels crush, and sometimes things can explode!

Construction workers build everything from homes to schools to offices. But let's see how the tallest buildings, **skyscrapers**, are made!

Big bang!

Demolition (say *dem-UH-lish-un*) experts get paid to smash things! They are in charge of safely destroying buildings. Some buildings aren't safe or are too old. They need to be knocked down to make room for new buildings.

jackhammer

There are many ways to destroy buildings. Small buildings are broken apart with noisy **jackhammers**.

Some large buildings are torn down with an **excavator** (say *ek-ska-VAY-tor*). Workers use the excavator's claw-like arm to rip apart walls and floors.

excavator

Sometimes workers use a wrecking ball to smash old buildings. The heavy ball swings from a tall **crane**. It crashes into the building again and again until it tumbles down.

wrecking ball

The quickest way to get rid of a tall building is to blow it up! **Demolition** experts place **explosives** in a building. When everyone is far away, a signal sets the explosives off. Kaboom!

DID YOU KNOW?

First the bottom floors of a building blow up. Then the top floors crash down, like a house of cards! Once the dust settles, all that's left is a pile of **rubble**.

Get to work!

The boss on a building site is the **site manager**. The site manager says which workers, machines, and supplies are needed each day.

blueprints

Site managers read the **blueprints** to keep the builders' jobs in order. They check that everyone's work is done right and on time.

Monster machines

The land must be cleared to make room for a new building. That's the backhoe operator's job. These big machines roar into action!

backhoe

Operators push foot pedals or
buttons to make their machines
move. A joystick controls the
machines actions.

Bulldozers have a curved blade on the front. They shove heavy things and smooth the ground. Bulldozers run on tracks so they won't get stuck.

track

Once the land is cleared, **excavators** roll in. The huge bucket digs holes for the **foundations** of buildings. **Skyscrapers** need strong foundations so they won't fall over.

The bed, or back, of a dumper truck is filled with soil and rocks. The drivers take the load to the dumping site. The front of the bed is lifted. Everything crashes out of the back.

bed

DID YOU KNOW?

A normal dumper truck can carry enough sand to fill 34 sandpits. But monster dumper trucks could fill 1,150 sandpits!

Skeleton walkers

Welders make the inside frames of **skyscrapers**. Sparks fly when they **weld** together the steel "skeletons" of the buildings.

safety net

Welders have dangerous jobs. They work on beams high up in the air. But they wear safety belts that catch them if they fall. Nets catch materials that may accidentally drop.

Liquid stone

Concrete is used for the building's **foundation** and walls. Workers make moulds to hold the concrete. Lorries bring soft concrete to the site.

concrete

Workers use pumps to pour the mushy concrete into the moulds. Then they smooth it out with long, flat rakes. It dries as hard as rock.

Knock on wood

Carpenters don't just use hammers and nails. They use power tools such as electric drills, saws, and sanders. Sawdust flies when they're at work!

saw

Some of these tools can be dangerous. Never use them without an adult to help you.

nail gun

Most carpenters use nail guns. The nail gun uses air to shoot nails into the wood.

Bright idea

Electricians wire up electricity in new buildings. Electricity powers heating, cooling, lights, phones, computers, smoke alarms, and many other things.

Like many workers on a building site, electricians wear a special belt to keep all their tools handy.

Could you work on a building site?

Building workers need to be able to follow directions. They should be good at working with their hands. Everyone has to work as a team.

DID YOU KNOW?

The tallest **skyscraper** is the Burj Khalifa. It is almost 1 kilometre (more than ½ mile) tall! It took more than 7,500 building workers to build it.

Glossary

blueprint drawn plan showing how a building needs to be made

bulldozer machine used to push heavy things

carpenter worker who makes or repairs wooden things

concrete soft building material that dries hard

crane machine used to lift and carry heavy things

demolition destroying something on purpose

electrician person who wires up electricity in a building

excavator a machine that digs or carries materials

explosive material used to break things apart with force

foundation underground part of a building that keeps it strong

jackhammer a large drill used to break things up

joystick a lever that controls a machine

rubble pieces of things that have been broken apart

site manager person in charge of workers on a building site

skyscraper a very tall building

weld using heat to melt together metal pieces

Find out more

Books to read

Diggers and Dumpers, Jayne Parsons
(Dorling Kindersley, 2005)

Machines at Work: On the Building Site, Ian Graham
(QED Publishing, 2006)

The Usborne Book of Big Machines, (Usborne, 2008)

Websites to visit

http://www.jcbexplore.com/
Find out how JCB excavators and other machines work.

http://www.kenkenkikki.jp/special/e_index.html
Learn about building equipment, with games
and videos.

http://www.pbs.org/wgbh/buildingbig/
Explore skyscrapers and what it takes to build them.

Index